2011

love ya! x

OVER 100 DARING & DEVIANT FETISH SEX TIPS

THIS IS A CARLTON BOOK

Text and design copyright ©
Carlton Books Limited 2008

This edition published by
Carlton Books Limited
20 Mortimer Street
London W1T 3JW

ISBN 978 1 84732 202 9

Printed and bound in Malaysia

Senior Executive Editor: Lisa Dyer
Senior Art Editor: Gülen Shevki-Taylor
Design: Zoë Dissell
Production: Kate Pimm

OVER **100**
DARING
& DEVIANT
FETISH
SEX **TIPS**

LISA SUSSMAN

CARLTON
BOOKS

Fetish Fun

When it comes to sex, there's something weird, wild and wonderful for everyone out there – from tickling torture to dressing head-to-toe in latex. Hey, as long as it's between two (or more) consenting adults, what's the harm in experimenting?

In fact, research shows that there's every reason to celebrate your secret desires. Getting **frisky with your fantasies** says a lot about your lust level. The more you're open to getting bold between the sheets, the more buzz you're likely to get from your bang. So the occasional randy romp in the bedroom (or outside of it) can actually be a great way to avoid a rut in your rutting. Plus the whole act of exploring your secret desires can cement your connection with your lover, which can – you got it – make for more out-of-body, melting sexperiences.

Whether you're a hard-core fetishist or simply curious, read on for easy ways to indulge in a little bit of what you fancy. It's as easy as reciting your A-B-C's.

A IS FOR AIR SUPPLY

Some people get **dizzy with pleasure** when you cut their air supply. Beginners can try shallow rapid breathing while they play. To bring it up a notch, try gently giving your lover's neck small pulsating squeezes as you lock lips. As their air is cut off, they can feel sensation more intensely. For hardcore asphyxiation aficionados, there are full-head latex hoods, but this is high-risk and can cause death.

2

A IS FOR ARMPITS

Axillists know that the ultra-thin skin in this area makes it a **natural hot spot**. Stroke it. Tickle it. Massage it. Lick it. Sniff it. To be a true pit lover, skip the deodorant and shave and get off on each other's natural odour.

A IS FOR AURAL SEX

Moriaphiliasts (who get aroused by telling dirty jokes) may take it to the extreme, but **dirty talk** is an easy no-risk way to get risqué. Start with a G-rated vocabulary, then build toward XXX. Instead of murmuring incoherently, get specific: 'Your mouth feels so warm and wet.' Gradually introduce your more graphic thoughts.

Get your lover in on the action by asking what they want you to do to them. Even if you know exactly what they want you to do, don't do it until they specifically ask – **beg** – you to do what they want. You'll soon have them speaking your lingo.

B IS FOR BLING

Make an undercover sexy fashion statement and **adorn your body** with sparkly nipple charms, clips, shields or earrings, pearl thongs or G-strings, belly jewels, penis or clit bells and clips, belly button clips or rings and back-belly chains. Your friends will wonder what you're smiling about.

5

B IS FOR BODY ART

Turn your flesh into an **erotic work of art** with body paints, henna stains or tattoos (temporary or permanent). Try flavoured paints and lick off your masterpieces. Scribble naughty thoughts and sexy sketches. Don't forget to take pictures.

B IS FOR BLUE

Make pornography part of your romantic routine. Don't just be a passive watcher, **use the images as inspiration** and try re-enacting the smuttier bits, scene by scene. Is that for me, Big Boy?

7

B IS FOR BOOTY LOVE

8

The anus is crammed with all sorts of feel-good ultra-sensitive nerve endings. Here's how to get inside.

Before any bottom games, play by the rules:

- Groom. Cut and file all your **nails**. Wash – and not just behind your ears. You may not want to go the whole hog and evacuate the entire area with an enema, but at least make sure things are **squeaky clean** with warm water and a gentle soap.
- Get kitted out. No matter how clean you get, the bottom is a breeding ground for bacteria. Using **latex** – either gloves (the kind doctors wear, available from most large pharmacies), a condom or dental dam – will help prevent infection.

Juice up. The anus has no natural **lubrication**, so you'll need to use lots and lots and lots of lube. The crème de la crème are gels made specifically for bottom play. But whichever grease you choose, make sure it's not oil-based (which dissolves latex). Get it all over your hand, the back of your hand, between your fingers. Make a huge mess. And keep applying it as you go. Maintain your site. Never go from anus to mouth, or anus to vagina, without **washing** carefully (and changing your latex) in between.

9

10

Get in position:

- Kneeling on your knees and elbows **'doggy style'** will make for easy access.
- Standing **bent over at the waist** creates a wide opening.
- If you prefer to **lie on your back**, draw your knees up to your chest and slip a pillow under your hips for a smoother landing.

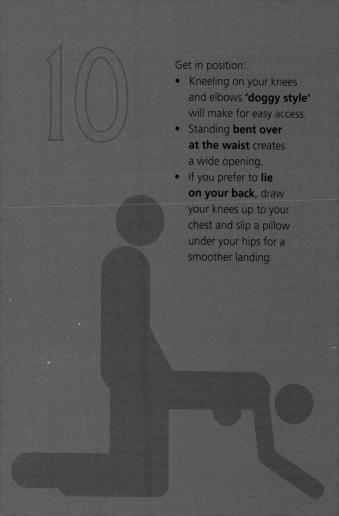

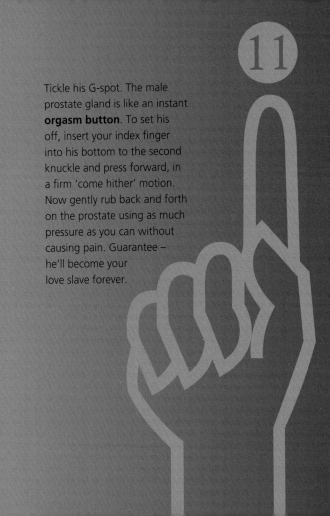

Tickle his G-spot. The male prostate gland is like an instant **orgasm button**. To set his off, insert your index finger into his bottom to the second knuckle and press forward, in a firm 'come hither' motion. Now gently rub back and forth on the prostate using as much pressure as you can without causing pain. Guarantee – he'll become your love slave forever.

11

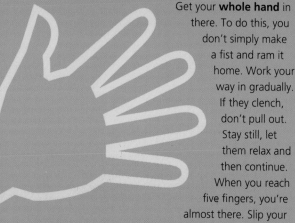

Get your **whole hand** in there. To do this, you don't simply make a fist and ram it home. Work your way in gradually. If they clench, don't pull out. Stay still, let them relax and then continue. When you reach five fingers, you're almost there. Slip your knuckles inside, folding your thumb 'inside' your fingers to form a fist. Now the fun begins – rotate and rock your hand in place until you cause an explosion.

TIP: Work your own backdoor. Some people can cause their own **big bang** by rhythmically contracting and relaxing their sphincter muscles.

13

Play **'Hide the Sausage'**.
Men love the ultra-tight
fit of anal sex.

14

Kiss ass. **Massage, kiss and lick**
your lover's lower back, thighs,
hips and cheeks as you gradually
make your way towards their back
hole. Widen your tongue to apply
pressure over the entire outside
area. Suck on the perineum (the
area between the anus and the
genitals). Now flatten it to push
against their opening. Slowly work
the tip of your tongue inside and
wiggle it around
in small
circles. Rinse
and repeat.

15

Toy with it. Use a small dildo or vibrator to get a back buzz on. Use your hand to work their other bits at the same time. Be prepared to **hold on for dear life**. See Tip 94 for more playthings.

16

C IS FOR CHASTITY BELT

It may seem odd to include abstinence in a book on sex, but there is something undeniably hot about enforced chastity. The more you can't have it, the more you want it. *Now.* You can **buckle up** for a day or for weeks (invest in a higher-end belt which will have toilet-friendly features).

C IS FOR CORSET TRAINING

The corset is to nudity what foreplay is to sex. No other garment is so erotic because none has as loaded an effect on the female form.

A corset will hold you in and boost you up for an amazing streamlined appearance. It makes any bust have **cleavage** to die for. Not to mention just slipping into one makes you want to **meow like a sex kitten.**

18

Today's corsets come in all sorts
of materials, from PVC to denim and
can be worn under just about
anything. But invest in a
good fit – the point is to
add emphasis to your
own sexy curves, not
to be restrained (unless
that oh-so-tight feeling
is part of your love gig).
No matter what, your boobs
should not be so lifted that
you're knocking them with your chin
and you shouldn't tighten the laces
to the point where you are passing out
or your belly bulges. Once you're in,
leave it on to add a wenchy slant to
your lovemaking.

D IS FOR DISCLAIMERS

Before you begin to trip the light fantastic or book a visit to the wild side of sex, you need to **talk with your partner** to make sure you are both on the same page. Also know that any type of experimentation is potentially dangerous – yes, that's part of the thrill. But it doesn't mean common sense should fly out the window – these games are more fun when you play safe.

19

D IS FOR DOGGING

Shift your sex play into high gear with a reckless fasten-your-seatbelt-romp in the backseat of a parked car while others watch from the outside. There are dogging websites to post when and where the **public showcase** will occur. Switch on your interior light when you're ready to start the show. Just be careful not to accidentally release the handbrake.

D IS FOR DOLLS

Guys like to play with dolls too. The queen of **synthetic love** is the Realdoll (www.realdoll.com) by Abyss Creations. Each Realdoll has a hinged jaw, soft silicone teeth and nipples that 'can withstand approximately 400 per cent elongation before tearing'. Although a high-priced option, the dolls are made of solid silicone, just like real pornstars.

21

E IS FOR ELECTRICITY

You can get an extra charge out of sex by clamping your genitals to an electrode and turning up the voltage. Or take the safer route and invest in a **Violet Wand**, a nineteenth-century-style medical device that stimulates those inner muscles with an electric current. The sensation is like having your lover lightly drag their fingertips over your skin and then that feeling is amplified by electrifying the touch so that tiny static sparks erupt from their fingertips. Just don't try it in the bathtub.

If you want to reduce your carbon footprint, you can make your loveplay buzz with erotic electricity by rubbing your feet on a **shag carpet** while tango-ing tongues.

F IS FOR FEED THE KITTY

Is your love life feeling a little vanilla lately? Add flavour to your sexual favours with some munchies. Sausages and unpeeled bananas and cucumbers all double up as **delicious dildos**.

24

Run an **ice cube** up and down and all around, and watch him melt. Or let the drips do the work.

25

Hit your sweet spot
and turn your bodies
into delicious
dessert buffets.
Cover each
other with gooey
gloopy foods such as **whipped cream,
ice cream and chocolate sauce** and
lick off. In fact, using marshmallow mush,
peanut butter and other gooey groceries
to make sex tasty is so common, it's got its
own name and website: www.splosh.co.uk.
There are two types of sploshers:
silly slapstick ones who throw
cream pies at each other
and sexy, food-as-foreplay
9½ Weeks devotees.
You choose.

26

27

Finish up with an Altoid. These curiously strong mints are infamous for boosting mouth sex into the stratosphere because the peppermint oil gives you that **powerful icy-hot feeling**. Tuck a few between your cheek and gum, or crunch them up completely (to prevent nasty abrasions from cut mints) for a whole mouthful of that minty goodness. Bon appétit!

28

G IS FOR GOTHIC

You don't have to live on the dark side to get the sexy appeal of occasionally going Goth. All it takes to transform yourself into a creature of the night is a black corset, a black bustle, black nail polish, a heavy dose of black eyeliner, some chain jewellery, a black leather jacket and a painted-on birthmark in the shape of a snake. For a real authentic touch, add white face powder. Enjoy your newfound menacing air by **ordering him to lie still** while you nibble at his neck.

G IS FOR GLOVES

True glove fetishists can get off on wearing a regular pair of pink rubber mitts and washing dishes. But you don't have to do housework to dip your pinkies into this kind of erotic play. **Throw down the gauntlet by slipping into a pair of elbow-length gloves.** Snug and sexy, you can get them in everything from silk to latex. Some varieties are also fingerless. Work your new digit-wear into your love scene by giving him a full-body gloved rubdown (take care how hard you squeeze – silk stains easily!).

G
IS FOR
GUSHER

Enough working of her G-spot (that spongy bump on the front of her vaginal canal about a finger's length in) will make some women come so hard that they spout fluid – which is not pee – much as he does. Some babes won't come to the orgasm party any other way. If he seems reluctant to put in the extra work, tell him that at least he'll know you're not faking it when you climax. The challenge is on!

30

H IS FOR HAIR

Judging from the number of pages catering for hair fascination – www.hairtostay.com, www.hairydivas.com, www.mylovedhairy.com (to name just a few of the more tame sites) – **hirsute babes are ultra-hot** in certain circles. But plaits, bunches and pigtails are also making the final cut.

TIP: If it's long lush locks that you're into, climb on top during sex and seductively brush your tresses back and forth across his body during sex. After, let him give you a shampoo and rinse.

H IS FOR HOOTERS

It's a fact: 99.99% of men are obsessed by breasts. But true **tit-elation** is when all it takes are a few bust-out moves to make those mounds quiver. For breast in show, slip into a push-up bra. Strut your stuff and watch him howl like a dog.

Make a sandwich by **slipping his hotdog between your top buns** and moving gently from side to side while he thrusts back and forth. For extra juice, add a squirt of lube. The friction will make him ask for seconds.

34 Adorn your breast self for what the best boobs are wearing these days (see also Tip 5). Or slip on a front-opening bra, **straddle him** and then pop the girls out onto his waiting mouth.

35 Skip the nipple. The top, bottom and sides of your breasts are actually where all the **ultrasensitive** nerve action is.

I IS FOR I SPY

Voyeurism comes from the French word *voir*, meaning 'to see'. While secretly spying on someone is a crime, sneaking peeks at **your lover getting off** is like a step-by-step of their favourite way to have sex.

36 Start up close and personal. Ask them to masturbate in bed while you watch, side by side. Then tell them you want to see them do it again – this time from a distance.

Try having them touch their body in front of the window while you peer in from the outside. They'll get a rush from having their own personal peeper while you feel like you're getting a free **peep show**.

38

J IS FOR JAPAN

Welcome to Tokyo, the world's most fetish-friendly city. Fetish clubs are on every corner: they've got run-of-the-mill girls in green goo, groin kicking, ear cleaning, nude washing, breast touching, stewardesses… and then there are the local specialties: **ganmen kookegi** (face attack), **nyotaimori** (eating off a naked woman), **unagi** (putting eels in a woman) and **ha daisuki** (a dental exam, where the 'porn' features fully clothed women getting their teeth checked).

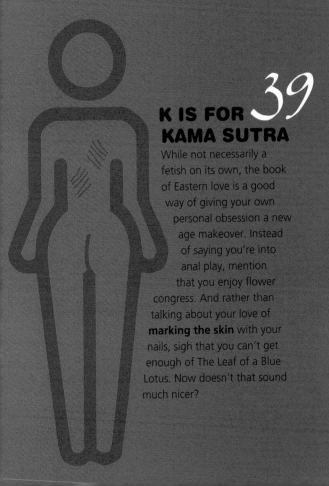

K IS FOR *39* KAMA SUTRA

While not necessarily a fetish on its own, the book of Eastern love is a good way of giving your own personal obsession a new age makeover. Instead of saying you're into anal play, mention that you enjoy flower congress. And rather than talking about your love of **marking the skin** with your nails, sigh that you can't get enough of The Leaf of a Blue Lotus. Now doesn't that sound much nicer?

40

K IS FOR KICKING ASS

Here's the deal: A favourite femme fantasy is to order their men around in bed like slaves and **spank them, smack them** and even penetrate them with a strap-on. And one of his happiest headtrips is to lay back and be told what to do (possibly because he's dog-tired with performing all the time). Let's get these crazy couples together.

K IS FOR
KNICKERS

Don't get sniffy if your lover takes a deep whiff of your undies. The French know the sexy power punch of Pepe le Peu briefs – according to one survey, 40% of Frenchmen and 25% of Frenchwomen do not change their underwear every day.

K IS FOR
KOKIGAMI

Like origami, only sexier. This is the Japanese art of wrapping the penis in a decorative paper costume, such as a dragon or a goose (see Tip 38 for more inscrutable ideas).

L IS FOR LATEX, LEATHER AND RUBBER – OH, MY!

Latex, leather, rubber, vinyl, patent leather, PVC… these are a few of a rubberist's favourite things. It's not just the skintight shiny look – it's the **feeling of being enclosed** that makes these materials hands-down sexy. Here's how to suit up for every occasion.

43

For daily wear, there are cropped shirts, dresses and skirts – all worn as **snug and short** as possible to show off your curves. Pants are a good option for both sexes, as are vests.

To whip things up, go for something backless to reveal your luscious bottom. Or throw on a pair of leather panties (crotchless, natch) and matching bra or a bra harness and a G-string or thong. **Complete the look** with fitted long gloves, stockings (some have lacings) and garters. Guys can slip into crotchless chaps, a G-string leather pouch or leather briefs with a cut-away section for his meat and two veg to peek through.

44

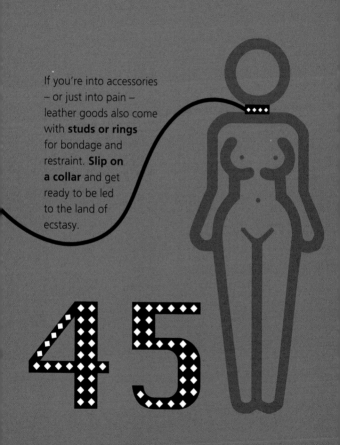

If you're into accessories – or just into pain – leather goods also come with **studs or rings** for bondage and restraint. **Slip on a collar** and get ready to be led to the land of ecstasy.

45

To hell with it – just go all out and slip into a full-body catsuit. Purr-fect. Or try the budget option of **paint-on, peel-off liquid latex** (www.l8tex.com), which you can use like body paint (you can also paint it over clothing). It comes in a rainbow of colours as well as clear for that shiny enclosed naked look. Pour it on and see it dry within minutes (faster if you use a hairdryer).

These materials are like a **second skin** and so getting into them is going to require a certain degree of prep – powder or lube your body before you get dressed. Also, none of this stuff is exactly what you would call 'breathable' – so unless you're also into body smells (see also Tip 2), load up on the deodorant.

48

Become a looner. Under the premise that if a latex catsuit is sexy, a latex balloon is sexier – and cheaper – some people enjoy overinflated balloons rubbed against their genitals. **Pop!**

49

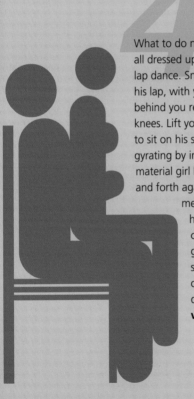

What to do now that you're all dressed up? Give him a lap dance. Snuggle onto his lap, with your hands behind you resting on his knees. Lift your ankles up to sit on his shoulders. Start gyrating by inching your material girl bum back and forth against his erect member. If you have something crotchless on, go ahead and slip him in and out of you to drive him **wild with desire.**

L IS FOR LIGHTS! CAMERA! FETISH ACTION!

You don't need to go for bad porn to enjoy kinky sex. Match your fetish to the great movie moment in these general releases.

For **cross dressing and body binding**, rent *Shakespeare in Love*.

Pivotal scene: Fast forward 45 minutes to the moment where Shakespeare unbinds his boy-love to discover the femme fatale underneath.

51

For **babydoll dress-up**, rent *The Lover*.

Pivotal scene: After 40 minutes of yearning, pigtailed 18-going-on-15-year-old Jane March throws herself at an older Chinese man and spends the rest of the movie mostly naked.

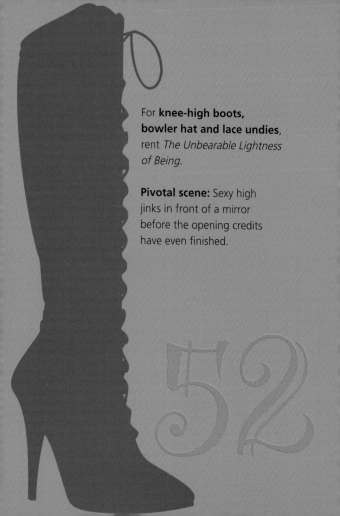

For **knee-high boots, bowler hat and lace undies**, rent *The Unbearable Lightness of Being*.

Pivotal scene: Sexy high jinks in front of a mirror before the opening credits have even finished.

52

For a **take-charge babe**, rent *Species*.

Pivotal scene: Blazing-hot alien babe steals a hotel key and practically rapes dorky scientist, tearing his pants off and riding him like a baffled bronco. The spikes that sprout from her back after the love-in are just gravy.

54

For **voyeurism**, rent *Henry and June*.

Pivotal scene: Luscious minx and hubby visit a bordello that specializes in 'exhibitions', and pay for a private viewing of a statuesque blonde and a passive brunette getting busy.

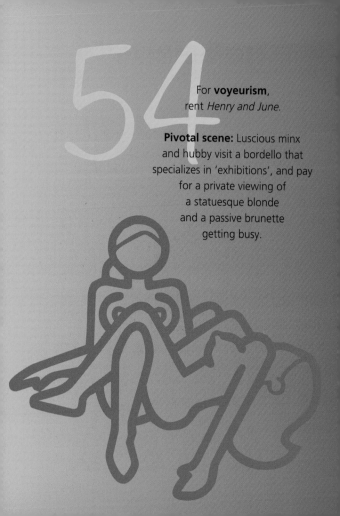

For **fit-to-be-tied bondage, part 1**, rent *Cat People*.

Pivotal scene: Inbred cat chick entices her zookeeper-lover to lash her limbs to a wooden bedframe so she won't slice him to pieces when the claws come popping out. Shot with excruciating slowness and plenty of full-frontals, it's the mother of all bondage scenes.

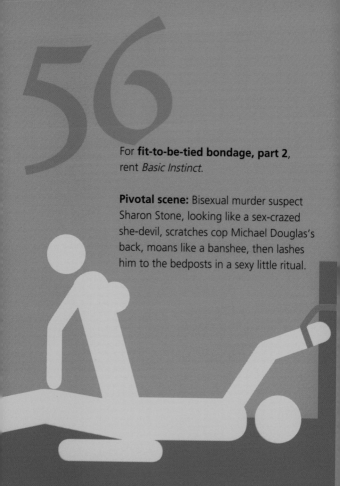

56

For **fit-to-be-tied bondage, part 2**, rent *Basic Instinct*.

Pivotal scene: Bisexual murder suspect Sharon Stone, looking like a sex-crazed she-devil, scratches cop Michael Douglas's back, moans like a banshee, then lashes him to the bedposts in a sexy little ritual.

For an **everything-but-the-kitchen-sink collection of fetishism**, rent *9½ Weeks.*

Pivotal scene: You choose.

For **lesbians, vampires and lesbian vampires**, rent *The Hunger*.

Pivotal scene: Catherine Deneuve licking a rapturous Susan Sarandon like an ice-cream cone.

59

For **hot, dripping wax**,
rent *Body of Evidence*.

Pivotal scene: Madonna gets
medieval on Willem Dafoe,
dripping hot wax onto his skin,
and then pouring a soothing
champagne salve on his
privates and licking it off.

L IS FOR LOCATION, LOCATION, LOCATION

Simply doing the deed somewhere other than your bed can give your romp a kinky edge. But exhibitionists get a headrush from the possibility of being caught in public with their knickers in a twist. Read on for the best places to fool around (along with tips on how not to end up in jail).

- **Make it a desk job:** Do it in your office. Or better yet, your boss' office. But be prepared to do it in the dole (unemployment) office afterwards!
- **Work it out:** Hit the gym. The calf-raise machine, the hip stretcher and the abs board all lend themselves to several hundred muscle moves while the sauna will give your play a steamy edge.
- **Choose your floor:** Any lift (elevator) will do but look out for those equipped with security cameras.
- **Window-shopping:** Go to a shop that has large private fitting rooms and try it on.
- **Public toilets:** Join the parade of celebs who've been caught washing more than their hands.
- **Rush hour:** The Japanese have made a fine art of humping on the Metro. If underground isn't your thing, a crowded bus will work equally well – just make sure you know whose bum you're rubbing against.

Like whipping off a tablecloth without disturbing the place settings, taking off your underwear in public can be tricky. It helps if you're already dressed to thrill – **go commando** and wear easy-access clothes like loose trousers (him) and a skirt or dress (her).

61

M IS FOR MIND YOUR MANNERS

A fetish party is like any get-together – the simplest way to fit in is to do like your mum taught you and behave politely. There will be people right in front of you who are doing very sexual things. They're doing them for *their* pleasure, not yours. Stay away from the action unless invited to participate – and a glance in your direction does not constitute an invitation. No heckling. Even if you want to lob a compliment their way, wait until the action is over.

M IS FOR MUCKY PUPS

If you're into getting down and dirty during sex with oily goo, soapy water or any slimy sloppy stuff that strikes your fancy, welcome to the world of **WAM: wet and messy fun** (for the ultimate info, click on www.geocities.com/gungesurvey/wamlinks.html). Adding some much-needed class, **Wetlook** deals with wet, elegant clothes. At the other end of the spectrum is **Gunge**, which covers you in food and pretty much anything but bodily excretions (see also 'sploshing' in Tip 24).

63

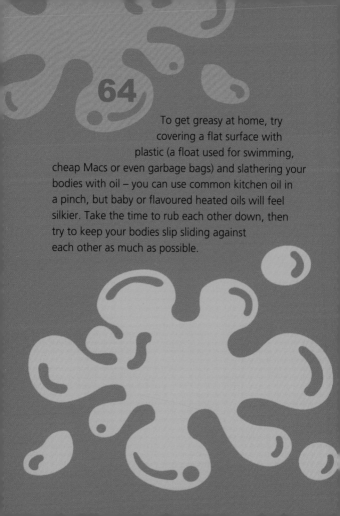

64

To get greasy at home, try covering a flat surface with plastic (a float used for swimming, cheap Macs or even garbage bags) and slathering your bodies with oil – you can use common kitchen oil in a pinch, but baby or flavoured heated oils will feel silkier. Take the time to rub each other down, then try to keep your bodies slip sliding against each other as much as possible.

M IS FOR MUMMIES

Proper merinthophiliasts wrap each other up with clingfilm (plastic wrap), pallet wrap or elastic veterinary wrap. But since novices tend to overlook small details – like breathing holes, a simpler option for the achieving a tight feeling is to roll your lover up tightly in a blanket (preferably one made of breathable material).

66

N IS FOR NAKED PICTURES

Seeing what you look like in the heat of pash may help you overcome any fears that your film will end up on YouTube (of course that may be part of the excitement). If you're going for an artistic look, opt for low lighting. If porn imagery is more your thing, make it light and bright – and be sure the sheets look at least a year old.

N IS FOR NASOLINGUS

Nose sucking. God bless!

67

O IS FOR OVERSIZED

According to the US National Association to Advance Fat Acceptance (NAAFA), around 15% of you would prefer to have a full-figured sex partner. The reason? There's **more to love**. Even the morbidly obese are eye-candy for a group called Fat Admirers, with whom they indulge in fantasies of being force-fed.

P IS FOR PIERCINGS

Piercing your nipples, navels, eyebrows, clitoris hoods, penises and labia turn them from mere body parts to 24/7 erotic zones. To make your markings the MVP (most valuable player) in your sex games, have your lover lavish them with **tongue love**. If it's your tongue that's been made into a sex stud, use it like an extra digit, running it over your mate's most sensitive bits. (If you love the look but hate the hole, check out B for Bling (Tip 5) for ways to dress up your bits and pieces without using a needle.)

Q IS FOR QUICK-CHANGE ARTIST

There's nothing as hot as being yourself – except possibly being yourself being somebody else.

70

Nurse, Barbie, nun, **secretary**, schoolgirl, robot, the military, teacher or student, lesbian French maid, housewife – exploring those alter-egos hanging around behind-the-scenes in your erotic fantasies can be a fun and fulfilling way to uncover what turns you on. Remember, you're not going for a Golden Globe here – just great sex.

71

Role-playing doesn't have to be scary master/slave rape scenes – unless, of course, that's your fantasy. Start off with **something simple**, like getting a makeover at the cosmetic counter of any department store. It's usually free and the look they come up with is often a cross between teenage slut and middle-aged matron. Or slip into some **lacy lingerie** outside of your usual wardrobe choice. Even if it's not your style, wearing it will make you feel like a different person in bed (read: sexy and empowered). Or pretend to be strangers having anonymous sex.

Other popular skits that can add more spunk to your sex are: doctor and patient ('It's time for your pelvic exam'), **road police officer and naughty motorist** (handcuffs and a watergun come in handy here), cheerleader and player ('Wanna play with my pom-poms?'), headmistress and pupil ('You deserve 40 whacks'), boss and PA ('Your assignment for today…'), and stripper and client (remember to pack some paper money for lap dances).

R IS FOR RAZOR'S EDGE

Calling all (hair) losers – some women love rubbing
a man's bald head while in a passionate embrace.
More men enjoy rubbing a woman's bald honeyspot.
The best – and hottest – way to **lose those short
and curlies**, wherever they're located, is with a razor.
Before you start, trim the hair short and close with
scissors or a beard trimmer and apply a thick
layer of moisturizing lotion after you're
done shaving. Nicks are painful, so
make sure you're sober when
you try this. And don't
follow up with
aftershave.

73

R IS FOR RESOURCES

You are not alone. A like-minded sex fiend is just a mouse click away.

74

Log onto www.fetishlink.
co.uk, www.fetishalliance.
net or www.fetishbank.net
for all things fetish.

Sexy **outfits** galore are at www.bionictonic. co.uk/sex_toys/ thongs.html.

Shoe fetishists will find **stiletto heaven** at www.amberssecrets.com.

If it's **equipment** you're after, gloriabrame.com/kinkylinks/ fetishlinkindex.html and www.marquis. de has everything you need – and more. Ann Summers (www.annsummers. com), Blowfish (www.blowfish.com), LoveHoney (www.lovehoney.co.uk) and Sh! (www.sh-womenstore.com) have a less hardcore selection.

R IS FOR RUB-DOWN

The French, as usual, have a word for it: frottage. It means 'rubbing', and when it comes to sex, it's pretty self-explanatory. Frottage is, in its purest form, full-body, face-to-face, **crotch-to-crotch contact**. It may not be celebrated in videos and porn stories, and may not be talked about too much, but it's a lovely part of making out and can be a fully fledged art in itself. There's not even any technique to learn – just do what feels good and you've got it. Ooh la la!

S IS FOR SHOE-INS

There are people out there who will fondle, kiss, orally pleasure and have sex with shoes. They call it retifism. Women call it shopping. Either way, high-heeled shoes are seductive and scary at the same time. Nothing transforms a girl into a bona-fide dominatrix faster than slipping on an extra 15 cm (6 inches) of height. Plus those **stiletto spikes** can inflict a lot of damage. You'll have him kissing feet in no time (see also Tip 77). If you want to prolong his agony, give him a peep show with open-toed heels.

77

T IS FOR THIS LITTLE PIGGY

Feet are amazingly rich in nerve endings. All your bodily sensations are plugged into the parietal lobe of your brain. It just so happens that genitals and feet share a fence in this **sensory** neighbourhood. Show off your plates of meat with a pair of slingbacks (see Tip 76 for more ideas). When he's suitably panting, kick off the heels, place your foot firmly on his chest and demand a massage and pedicure. Don't forget to leave a tip.

T IS FOR THREE'S COMPANY

Based on the rationale that if one is fun, two will double the pleasure, the ménage à trois is a hot ticket item in the fetish world. But both men and women tend to fantasize more about inviting an extra babe between the sheets rather than a second Johnny-Come-Lately. It's okay if she **brings along a dildo or vibrator** to use on him as a party favour, but women seem to feel more comfortable – initially, at any rate – getting kinky with another gal pal. The post-game relationship recovery rate seems to depend on how much the Number One Girl was made to feel like a third wheel. If she gets to pick the potential ménage mate and start the party, she's more likely to enjoy a repeat episode.

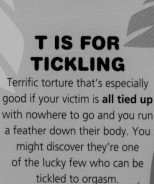

T IS FOR TICKLING

Terrific torture that's especially good if your victim is **all tied up** with nowhere to go and you run a feather down their body. You might discover they're one of the lucky few who can be tickled to orgasm.

U IS FOR UPSIDE DOWN

It's true; a rush of blood to the head **intensifies orgasm**. Pros use foot-suspension stirrups, but if you don't want to be caught hanging upside down from the door frame when your granny pops in unexpectedly, simply have sex sitting facing each other and lean your head back as things heat up.

U IS FOR UNIFORM

Who doesn't go crazy for a man in uniform or a woman dressed in a **cheerleader's outfit**? See Tip 70 for ideas on how to get into costume.

V IS FOR VAMPIRES

The extreme version of this fetish is using disposable scalpels and acupuncture needles to make the red stuff flow. But if this sort of sex play is not your idea of a bloody good time, restrict yourself to hickies. Sucking hard on the skin – especially in nerve-sensitive places such as the neck – can be **ghoulishly delicious**.

V IS FOR VIXEN

It's the ultimate femme fatale fantasy: red lipstick and long, red-painted fingernails. Run your scarlet talons up and down his back giving him long languorous smooches that leave **sexy smitten smudges** all over his face. It's the closest you'll get to adulterous sex without actually cheating.

W IS FOR WACKY
WILD WEB SEX

With just a modem and a horny dream, you can easily locate like-minded lovers of adventurous sex. The Internet lets you test the waters – say, by lurking in a chat room – before committing yourself. Just type your **favourite fetish** into your search engine and your hard drive will do the rest. If you do decide to jump in with both feet and make your virtual sex a reality, play it safe and always meet in a public place.

W IS FOR WIGGING OUT

There are burlesque wigs, Goth wigs, heart-shaped wigs, fluorescent wigs, Louis XIV wigs… and those are just for your pubic area.

The merkin started life in the 1600s as a way for prostitutes to **pretty up their honeypot** after shaving for vermin. Now it's become a fetishist's dream – decorating the (preshaved) pubic area with a wig of the week. Merkins can be attached with spirit gum or via a transparent G-string.

For a more public change, slip into a head wig. Trying on a different look can make you feel like another person – one more inclined to explore their wild side, perhaps. And the whole thing gives him the titillating feeling that he's cheating on you, especially if you take on a **new badass name** – like Bambi or Misty.

W
IS FOR
WATERSPORTS

This isn't about playing water polo in the nude. Golden showers – either being peed on or peeing on others – tends to be a guy thing. If this is something you're curious about, saying, 'Hey honey, **I want to piss on you**, bend over', is probably not the way to get your bedmate to play with you. You could ask to watch them pee and see how that goes down. One word of advice: try diluting the stuff by drinking lots of fruit juice first. It will smell a whole lot sweeter. She may even ask for a straw.

W IS FOR WAX PLAY

Go ahead, play with fire. It'll make your sex **sizzle**. Full-scale users cover themselves head-to-toe in a polished waxsuit, but all you need are a few melted drops to heat up your home fires.

Go no-frills – cheap, unscented white candles work better than the fancy-schmancy perfumed, coloured beeswax kinds for sexplay because they burn more slowly.

TIP 1: If he's a fuzzy wuzzy bear, he should shave first or plan to spend the rest of his life picking wax chunks off his body.

TIP 2: Oiling the skin before waxing makes removal easier later. Massage oils seem to stay cooler than baby oil, which gets hot under wax.

TIP 3: Tilt the candle slightly so the hot wax drops one tantalizing drip at a time.

TIP 4: Be very careful about lingerie – some items will melt or burn, sticking to the skin and causing serious burns. Anything with nylon, vinyl, PVC or patent leather would not get the firemen's seal of approval. Some artificial fingernails can melt at high temperatures too.

89 Try playing with temperatures – alternate between **hot wax and ice** for extremes that will drive your sweetie wild, or use a blindfold so everything comes as a surprise.

90 To get the more sensitive bits of the body like the nipples and the family jewels (his and hers) in on the action with all of the pleasure and none of the pain, run your finger along the edge of the candle so you get a wax-covered finger. Then let that finger **stroke and poke** where it will.

91

Smear your ride in **edible massage wax** and then polish their fenders with your tongue.

92

Don't trust him enough to let him pour hot melted wax on your naked skin? Then get your beautician to do it for you. Try a **Brazilian wax** (completely bald, front and back) – you lie on your back on the waxing table, obscenely holding your legs wide apart and up in the air like some porno hussy while the pussy stylist smooths gobs of warm gooey wax over your nether regions. It feels like heaven until the first r-r-rip!

X IS FOR XXX TOYS

Who says you can't buy kinky happiness? Here are a few of the more funky toys available at your local corner sex shop (see also Tip 74).

Anal beads: And the bead goes on. You stick these jewels in your bum and then pull them out again, one at a time.

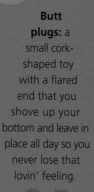

Butt plugs: a small cork-shaped toy with a flared end that you shove up your bottom and leave in place all day so you never lose that lovin' feeling.

Double-headed dildos:
Like the pushmi-pullyu, these have a head at each end so there are no fights over sharing. You can get them with the same size heads or one junior and one supersize.

Cock rings: A ring even a commitment-phobe will wear – who doesn't want a larger penis with a never-ending erection? High-end ones come with vibrators – now that's a joy buzzer!

Speculum: These come in handy for those doctor/patient scenes. Get the right size or else your role play will rapidly turn into an S&M scene.

Harness: These usually come with a dildo or vibrator so she can be the man of the house.

Ball gag: Some find the feeling of being gagged in this way incredibly arousing; others just enjoy the silence it guarantees. Ball gags are not 'one size fits all', so your best bet is one made from an easy-fitting jelly-like material. And make sure you agree on a hand signal for when the ball should come out.

100

Tweezer nipple clamps: A gentle introduction into the world of nipple love, these are fully adjustable and so won't hurt… unless you want them to. Even more fun – the nipples have to be fully hard before you can put them on.

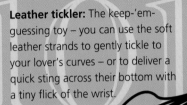

Leather tickler: The keep-'em-guessing toy – you can use the soft leather strands to gently tickle to your lover's curves – or to deliver a quick sting across their bottom with a tiny flick of the wrist.

102

Masks: Skip the Hannibal Lecter headgear. Instead, bring a silk scarf to bed. On second thoughts, bring a few silk scarves. Use them as blindfolds and straps. Then go ahead and have your wicked way.

Spanking paddle:
You'll be belting out 'Hurts So Good' when your lover gives you a smackdown. There are some scary-looking paddles available (spikes, anyone?), so save your money and use a ping-pong racquet instead. Mix pleasure with the pain by pausing between spankings and massaging their bottom with your hands.

Bondage tape: Sure, you could use duct tape, but this stuff is purposely made with a sexy shine and self-adhesive so that it won't stick to the body or get stuck in the hair. This means you don't have to worry about the tape self-tightening as your lover wriggles enticingly on your bed. It also means there won't be any undue pain when you finally remove it. You can use bondage tape to tie wrists, legs or ankles… or you can make like the pros and create some skanky new fetishwear: miniskirts, halter-tops, bras and panties are easily made with this stuff. When it's time for removal, you can use scissors or peel it off and reuse it again later.

Y IS FOR YOUCH!

Before starting, make sure you're **packing the right tools**. If he's knocking at your back door, make sure you have some lube ready and waiting. And if that cock ring is turning his baby-back blue, don't ruin future kinky opportunities by forcing him to forge on. Always check in to make sure you're both happy.

Z IS FOR ZZZZZ

Having sex with someone while they're
sleeping might be considered an assault.
But what if they're pretending to be asleep?
The person in make-believe dreamland gets the
anticipation of wondering where the next kiss or caress
is going to be placed on their naked 'sleeping' body while
the one starting the sex play gets to have total control over
everything, from the kind of foreplay to what position to put
their love schnoozer in. The hardest part of this charade
is staying still in the midst of a climax.
Wet dreams were never so
sweet.